Dundee Women's Trail

FALL IN
AND
FOLLOW ME

Take a walk in some great women's shoes...

Published 2008 by Dundee Women's Trail
PO Box 10277,
Dundee DD1 9TZ
www.dundeewomenstrail.org.uk

ISBN: 978-0-9558820-0-5

Contents

"THE SHE TOWN"

Women

don't appear much in history books. Generally it has been men who have held the positions of power and eminence – as they do today – while women work behind the scenes. But some, like Mary Slessor and Fanny Wright in this Trail, have become famous, and others have achieved much in science, the arts and social reform, and have promoted the cause of women in their own individual ways.

Dundee's coat of arms bears the lilies of the Virgin Mary, and the city was once known, when the jute trade was at its height, as "The She Town", in acknowledgement of women's prominence and economic independence. So it is fitting that, in this City of Discovery, we should discover some of the women who have helped to make it what it is.

This book is a companion to a trail of plaques in Dundee City Centre. The plaques commemorate the twenty-five remarkable Dundee women whose stories appear in this book. If you would like to follow the Trail, the fold out map at the back of this book will help you find out just where these amazing women lived, worked, battled and created

Left: Mill girls
Copyright © Dundee Heritage Trust, 2008

~ 5 ~

AGNES HUSBAND

1852 – 1929

Agnes Husband's story is interwoven with that of many others featured in this Trail. She was described in her obituary as, "...a pioneer in asserting the claims of women and their competence to participate in the administration of public affairs...". Assertions that still need making today, nearly 80 years after her death.

She was born in Tayport into a comfortable home; her father was a master mariner. She set up in business as a dressmaker. It was only later, when she was living at 69 Murraygate, that she decided to enter the world of public administration and stood for election to the Parochial Board (later called the Parish Council) as a Socialist candidate. At first she was unsuccessful, but in 1901 she was elected as one of the first two women members, the other being Mary Lily Walker (see plaque seventeen).

She worked hard on the Council, attending an average of 80 meetings a year, and there she managed to introduce a rather more humane approach to the needs of the poor. Then, about five years later, she was elected to the School Board, where she served as one of usually two women members out of thirteen, and continued until the year before her death. Again she was active in pressing for better care, and for a better quality of education for Dundee's children.

A prominent member of the Labour Party, Miss Husband also campaigned for women's suffrage: she must have been one of the older active suffragettes. Along with Emily Thomson (see plaque six) she was present at the formation of the moderate Dundee & East Fife Women's Suffrage Committee, but when the militant movement, the Women's Social & Political Union, arrived in Dundee she immediately joined up. The next year, 1909, she became president of the breakaway Women's Freedom League and a member of the National Executive. In this capacity she joined a deputation to Winston Churchill later that year - with little success. He made a speech that night against the League. As if all this wasn't enough, Miss Husband was also actively associated with the Distress Committee, the National Health Insurance Committee, the Juvenile Advisory Committee and the Departmental Committee on Industrial and Reformatory Schools. After the 1914–18 war she joined the executive committee of the Women Citizens' Association, and in 1926, at the age of 74, she was given the Freedom of the City. She had little patience with some of her weaker sisters. "Women grumble about things that should be done and are not done, and yet they stand aside and will not make the least little sacrifice to take up work which is a great deal more important than the work some of them waste their time over". But then, she had her younger sister Kitty to keep house for her. A busy lady, who perhaps would not have minded the label of do-gooder, hers is one of only two portraits of female councillors to hang in the City Chambers.

Previous page: Painted Portrait of Agnes Husband by Alec Grieve
Copyright © Dundee City Council, McManus Galleries and Museum, 2008

MARIOTE KER

16th century

Mariote Ker was made a burgess of the Royal Burgh of Dundee on the 12th November 1529 "by the king's request". The king in 1529 was James V, and he was only seventeen at the time, though he had been declared of full age at fourteen. Was she a member of his court? A superior servant? Did she lend or give him money? Or, given his reputation as the king who fathered more bastards than any other, did she show him other sorts of favour?

Whatever the reason, she was Dundee's first woman burgess: the second was not appointed for another 360 years. Election as a burgess gave Mariote important commercial advantages, as burgesses had monopolies in the production of goods such as bread, beer and clothes.

The ceremony would probably have taken place at the Tolbooth, which stood at the corner of Reform Street and High Street.

You'll find her plaque at Gardyne's Land, the only remaining building of Mariote's time left in Dundee – a medieval building for a medieval lady.

AN ANONYMOUS MAIDSERVANT

1872

A group of women to be reckoned with used to meet at the Thistle Hall in Union Street (now converted to flats). In 1872 there occurred an 'agitation of maidservants' unique in Britain. They were anonymous because they would have lost their jobs otherwise. But the nice thing was that in those days, unlike today, the press respected their anonymity.

In the late nineteenth century there were no trade unions for domestic servants in Scotland, though there were Friendly Societies for men on the west coast. But there was plenty to grumble about. The women met first in April that year, at Mathers Hotel in Murraygate (now demolished), and shortly afterwards at the Thistle Hall. By May the Dundee & District Domestic Servants Association had 200 members - perhaps 5% of all those working as live-in domestic servants in the area. Their chief demands were for shorter working hours and for the right not to wear uniform; they also hoped to establish their own servants' employment registry.

Meetings were widely reported throughout the UK and even in the USA. Verbatim newspaper reports of speeches give a picture of lively meetings, with women being openly scathing about their employers: "You know some of them are just set up with a little authority and they think they have the ball at their own feet and that they can kick it any way they like". However, the newspapers also made fun of the women's efforts, so they decided not to let reporters come to their meetings. This was probably a mistake, as publicity had been a big help in getting attention and gaining members. A further reason for 'lack of interest' was that "the mistress had carefully kept the papers out of the way of the servants lest they be indoctrinated with trade unionist principles". We know that they met with the Dundee Trades Council in November and discussed expanding to Broughty Ferry, but after that nothing more.

The next effort to unionise women domestic servants in Scotland was by one Jessie Smith, in Glasgow in 1912, but it failed and she went south. Ironically, the government enquiries set up in 1916 and 1918 repeated just what the women had said nearly fifty years before. So did this movement achieve anything? It has to be said there were no concrete results, but it did help make the public aware of the problems for domestic servants and less seriously, it certainly gave some women the chance to let off steam!

FRANCES WRIGHT

1795 – 1852

"Can Truth be dangerous?" the young Fanny asked her maths tutor. "It is thought so," he replied. This didn't much daunt her.

She was born at 136 Nethergate into a wealthy family, daughter of James, an accomplished and ardent republican and friend of Adam Smith, Thomas Paine and Lafayette. Orphaned at the age of 2½, she was brought up by an aunt in England. She got herself an excellent, though unusual, education and came to hold the same views as her father. She quarrelled with her aunt and returned to Scotland. At the age of eighteen, she published a short but learned book, "A Few Days in Athens", defending the Epicurean philosophy that life is here to be enjoyed, and blaming religion for many of society's troubles, which caused quite a stir. Then she read (in Italian) a history of the United States and was hooked: here was a country where freedom truly reigned! But did it exist? She didn't know, and had to look it up in an atlas. It did, and off she went with her younger sister Camilla, aged 23 and without a single acquaintance in that country. The British public at that time was very ignorant and prejudiced about America, so Fanny's published letters home were both successful and informative.

She then spent four or five years in Paris with Lafayette (causing "a wheen o' gossip") before returning to America in 1824. Disappointed that the USA had not lived up to the ideal of freedom in its constitution, she decided to try and put her own ideals into practice. She bought a farm near Memphis, Tennessee and settled slaves there, educating them and hoping that they could work out their freedom. Sadly, the project was ill-planned, and failed when she broke down from overwork and was ordered abroad for her health. Nevertheless, she was one of the very first people to discern the importance of the slavery question, and to try and solve it by agreement rather than conflict.

In Europe she made friends with Mary Shelley. She wrote to her about the Memphis experiment: "I have devoted my time and fortune to laying the foundations of an establishment where affection shall form the only marriage, kind feeling and kind action the only religion, respect for the feelings and liberties of others the only restraint and union of interest the bond of peace and security."

Back in the USA again, Fanny went to New Harmony, Indiana, to work on various socialist publications with the reformer Robert Owen, and she became famous as a lecturer, speaking in every major city and drawing huge crowds. A female lecturer was a great novelty, and Fanny's outspoken views on freedom for slaves, public education, free love and women's suffrage, and her attacks on the church, had sensational effect wherever she went. She was 5'10", erect and handsome. Her name became a household word, and John Stuart Mill described her as one of the most important women of his day. Even Owen, though he thought her conceited and impetuous, acknowledged her intellect, her courageous independence of thought and her willingness to make great sacrifices for conviction's sake.

When she was 36 she married Phiquepal D'Arusmont, but the marriage was not a success. She retired with her daughter to Cincinnati, Ohio and, plagued by ill health, was much less heard of in these later years. Bankrupted by D'Arusmont and estranged from her daughter, she died twenty years later poor and lonely, but her admirers kept fresh flowers on her grave for over a hundred years. Not until ten years after her death did Lincoln declare the abolition of slavery in the United States.

MARGARET FENWICK

1919 – 1992

"A doughty campaigner" is how Margaret Fenwick is described, and how, most likely, she would like to be remembered.

Margaret's early home was at the top of Lilybank and she went to Stobswell School. As soon as she could, she was out to work as an apprentice weaver at the SCWS Taybank Works. She was conscious of her rights from the very beginning. When she was only fifteen she discovered that older women doing the same work as herself were paid more: she demanded, and got, equal pay. She joined the Dundee & District Union of Jute & Flax & Kindred Textile Operatives, an organisation which had been founded about 20 years earlier by six women and which, unusually for the time, had equal numbers of men and women on its executive.

A fellow weaver remembers her as always standing up for their rights, even when they weren't aware they had a grievance. "She liked to hear herself! But she was a good friend, and always ready for a laugh." Andy, her husband, worked in the same mill, though he had to go into the army during the war. They had four children.

In 1960 she became assistant secretary of the union. The following year the union called its first all-out strike, marching round the town with banners. Margaret said: "I remember standing there crying. I was so proud of them all. Everybody said they'd never do it, and they did it." The women won a rise of 1% and Margaret continued campaigning for parity with men throughout her working life.

She moved to Jute Industries, to Mid Wynd Works and back to SCWS, always working as a weaver, until 1971 when she became the first woman General Secretary of a British trade union. A hefty, determined woman, with a perpetual cigarette, she did not take lightly to opposition,

though unlike her male predecessors she was prepared to work with employers on some issues. On a deputation to the City Chambers over rents, she got so angry with a Tory Councillor for insulting workers that it is said she rose from her seat and would have strangled him, had she not been restrained.

She served on various jute-related committees, and did much to improve health and safety as well as pay, and in 1973 her hard work was acknowledged with the award of an MBE. By 1979, with the jute industry in recession, she had retired. But she wasn't done yet: she continued to work on Industrial Tribunals and to serve as a JP. Of the Union she said: "I think I've left it a wee bit better than I found it, but there's still so much to be done".

The Union headquarters were at 93 Nethergate. In the 1980s the textile workers' unions were eventually absorbed into the TGWU.

ALICE MOORHEAD
EMILY THOMSON

Alice Moorhead 1868 - 1910
Emily Thomson c.1864 - 1955

Dundee's first women doctors were both brought up in India and they may have been introduced to each other there by another Dundee family of doctors, the Laings. It is more likely however that they met as medical students in Edinburgh. Although the Edinburgh medical school was not open to women until 1916, they both studied there extra-murally and then did their maternity qualification in Dublin. Alice was the daughter of a Brigade Surgeon, and followed a family medical tradition. Both women registered as doctors in 1891, two of only 101 women doctors then practicing in Britain.

In 1893 they opened their practice at 93 Nethergate, moving to 4 Tay Square by 1901 (both houses were owned by the Laings). They must have been successful GPs for they lived in some style, with housemaid, cook, chauffeur and car, one of the first cars in town. Dr Emily was Dundee's first woman driver.

As partners they complemented each other perfectly. The dainty Dr Alice worked mainly with the poor patients, both visiting, and holding a Saturday clinic for mill workers, while go-getter Dr Emily worked with the well-off and was more involved in other projects, like the founding of the Women's Hospital (later to become Elliot Road Hospital: see Mary Lily Walker, plaque seventeen) where she was appointed first Medical Officer. She was also to be seen at meetings of suffragettes. A young friend described them thus: "Dr Alice, fair, blue-eyed, soft-spoken, with a touch of Irish gaiety, adored by her patients" and "Dr Emily, vivid, dark, business-like, capable, inspiring confidence...". They were good friends too, for they went on holiday together.

But at the turn of the century it was not easy for a woman to become or practice as a doctor, and the life took its toll on Dr Alice. By 1906 she was said to be fading; she married a Dr Langwill in 1908 and went to live in Leith, but within two years she had died in childbirth. Dr Thomson moved to 22 Windsor Street, where she continued to practice until she retired in 1922. A few years earlier she had bought a house in Arbirlot, near Arbroath, where she lived with a daughter of the Lindsay grocery family. She collected antiques and works of art and lived to the ripe old age of 91. Visitors described her house as a treasure trove.

Alice and Emily's house in Tay Square has been pulled down, but a new surgery flourishes in the same spot.

An early female car driver – an unusual sight at the time!
Reproduced with kind permission of David Annand

MARY ANN BAXTER

1801 – 1884

A member of the leisured classes she may have been, but this lady was no slouch, and she certainly had a highly intelligent mind of her own. The Baxters were wealthy linen manufacturers and her father had the profitable naval contract for supplying canvas. So it may be supposed that Mary Ann grew up following the usual polite pursuits of young ladies of the period.

She was a member of the Congregational Church, and very devout. She never married, and as she and her brother David were the only two of the family with no children, they found themselves with "the means and opportunity to do good", and proceeded to give money away generously. Much went to the church and to missionary activity in New Guinea, where a river was named after her (the Baxter) and a steamer after her house (the Ellangowan).

By 1863 Baxter's was the largest linen firm in the world. Sir David was knighted, and he, Miss Baxter and their sister Eleanor donated Baxter Park to the people of Dundee. She took a lively interest in local affairs too, and her correspondence must have been voluminous. She never gave money away indiscriminately, and "while giving willingly she did not yield to further persuasion". In particular, she wouldn't help any charity bazaar, as she thought this form of giving "injurious to the pure spirit of Christian willinghood".

Then, at the age of 80, in association with lawyer Tom Boyd Baxter, a second cousin, she founded University College Dundee in 1881. At this time there were growing provincial demands for university education, and she followed the example of Manchester. She personally donated £140,000 of the £150,000 needed, and letters about the founding of University College show her to have had a clear idea of how she wanted her money spent. She objected strongly to some appointments and proposals, chose the site, chose the name 'University College' and produced her own draft of the constitution. She was insistent that [a] the college should not be absorbed by St Andrews, [b] it should have enough money and [c] it should teach every subject but divinity. It was to be "... a college for promoting the education of persons of both sexes and the study of science, literature and fine arts".

No one associated with the College should have to declare their religious opinions - a condition inspired perhaps by the fact that, until recently, non-conformists had been able to graduate only at London University. Mary Ann Baxter's life was quiet, and she was "remarkable for the unostentatious simplicity of her nature". It should also be noted that she was not overly rash in her giving; when she died she still had more than quarter of a million pounds to leave to her nephew!

Painted Portrait
Copyright © University of Dundee Archives, 2008

WILLIAMINA FLEMING

1857 - 1911

L ook at the stars! look, look up at the skies!
O look at all the fire-folk sitting in the air!
The bright boroughs, the circle-citadels there!

Gerard Manley Hopkins

Dundee has a fine record in astronomy, with the only public observatory in Britain. But Williamina Fleming did her stargazing in the United States.

Her father, who died when she was young, had a business at 62 Nethergate as a carver and printseller, and the family moved from home to home, finally settling in William Street. When she reached fourteen she became a pupil-teacher and then a regular teacher and, as far as is known, had no particular interest in stars. At twenty, she married James Orr Fleming and went to America with him to start a new life but the marriage was unhappy and within two years they had separated. Williamina, with her infant son Edward Pickering Fleming, got a job as housekeeper to Edward Pickering, Director of Harvard College Observatory and was soon working as a permanent member of the Observatory staff, doing copying and computing. By 1899 her "keenness of vision and clear and logical mind" had served to put her in charge of the photographic library, where plates were examined and indexed. This was a very new technique: in effect Mrs Fleming pioneered the classification of stellar spectra.

Altogether she classified 10,851 stars, which were listed in the Draper Catalogue of Stellar Spectra, published in 1890. In the course of her work she discovered 10 novae, 52 nebulae and 222 variable stars - a notable extension of the known heavens. She was a hard-working and strict, though not unpopular boss, and a football fan in her spare time. Her successor described her as an "extremely magnetic personality... her bright face, her attractive manner and her

cheery greeting with its charming Scotch accent will long be remembered". But there was another side to her character. Hoffleit (her biographer) wrote: "Sparkling and friendly as she was, her reputation as a strict disciplinarian lived after her, and as late as the 1930s elderly ladies who had worked with her in their youth still regarded her with awe". She was the first woman to hold a formal appointment at Harvard. In 1906 she was made an honorary member of the Royal Astronomical Society of London and was also honoured by France and Mexico, as well as in America, her adopted homeland. She was undoubtedly the leading woman astronomer of her day. On the rooftops above her plaque you can see our modern technology searching the skies!

LILA CLUNAS

1876 – 1968

Miss Lila Clunas (real name Maggie) was a small, quiet, kindly vegetarian, a teacher in Brown Street Public School. She doesn't seem very interesting? Read on!

Miss Clunas was born in Glasgow but spent her life in Dundee. She trained as a teacher at Moray House (Edinburgh), then came to teach in Dundee. A lifelong member of the Labour Party, she joined the suffrage movement in 1906, enrolling in the Women's Freedom League the following year. Her sisters, Elsie and Jessie, were members too. She wasn't a militant suffragette. On the other hand she was not at all quiet, being involved in meetings, and deputations, heckling and writing to the press. It is often thought that suffragettes were all middle class but this was far from the case in Dundee. "A meeting at 3.30 is an insult to the working women of this town," said Miss Clunas firmly.

In 1908 she was a member of a nine woman delegation to Prime Minister Asquith at Number 10. She took a swipe at him and was sentenced to three weeks, the first Dundee suffragette to be imprisoned in London. She went on hunger strike and was released early as "an act of clemency", but when she spoke of her experiences afterwards at a meeting chaired by Agnes Husband (see plaque one) she didn't sound too grateful. "If we are criminals we should be treated as such. If we are not we should be set free."

Undaunted, she continued to lead the chants of "Votes for Women!" to drown out hostile politicians. She was forcibly ejected from a Churchill election meeting and later, in 1914, from a Ramsay MacDonald meeting. Browse the old newspapers in the Local Studies Library in the Wellgate Library, Dundee if you want to read some of her sharp-tongued, witty letters.

For the second half of her life Miss Clunas lived in Broughty Ferry with her sister. She was co–opted to the Town Council in 1943, then elected in 1948, where she served until she was 88, taking a particular interest in education, libraries and parks. Articulate as ever, "Miss Clunas never spoke unless she had something to say but when she did she was apt to surprise her male colleagues by her logic and eloquence".

Not so boring then.

The former Brown Street Public School, now a public bar.
Copyright © GSR Photographic, 2008

Margaret Fairlie

1891 – 1963

LLD, MB, ChB St A, FRCS Ed, FRCOG, Emeritus Professor of Midwifery & Gynaecology. It is said that Dr Fairlie was as formidable as her string of initials. But then, no woman could have succeeded as a doctor at the beginning of the 20th century without considerable ability and determination. Only twelve years earlier it had been impossible for a woman to study in St Andrews, because the professor had ruled it was "positively indecent to lecture to a woman in physiology and anatomy".

Margaret Fairlie was born in Arbroath, graduated at St Andrews, then worked in Dundee, Perth and Edinburgh, before travelling to Manchester to learn specialist midwifery and gynaecology. At 28, she came as assistant to Professor John Kynoch at Dundee Royal Infirmary (DRI) and St Andrews University. She also had her own private practice, was visiting gynaecologist to all the hospitals in Angus and North Fife and qualified as a surgeon. At one point she was engaged to be married to a professor of surgery, but he died.

1926 was a significant year in her life. She visited the Marie Curie Foundation in Paris and saw the potential of radium in the treatment of cancer, becoming a pioneer in this field. She had her own small supply of radium and she is said to have buried it for safety in the Sidlaw Hills on the outbreak of war in 1939. The next year she was appointed as the first ever woman professor of midwifery at St Andrews, a post she held for fifteen years. When she retired from DRI, she was made Consultant Emeritus of Midwifery – another first for a woman.

Some of her many achievements included the introduction of vaginal cytology, the forerunner of smear tests, and a part responsibility for the beginnings of Dundee's teaching hospital. In her private life she achieved acclaim as a watercolourist.

Dr Fairlie was an elegant woman, viewed with respect tinged with awe, and was known as "Madam" by both students and colleagues. A patient reports being terrified of her. Nevertheless, the British Medical Journal describes her thus: "There was no more popular teacher, nor one whose teaching was more helpful.... Her sense of humour and her quick repartee never failed her, nor her courage.... her charm and hospitality were well known... her capacity for work was prodigious".

Dr Fairlie and Rebecca Strong (plaque eleven) are celebrated opposite the gates of the former DRI.
Copyright © Dundee City Council, Local Studies Library, 2008

Rebecca Strong

1843 – 1944

Mrs Strong was only connected with Dundee for four or five years, but in that short time made a long-lasting difference to the health and happiness of its citizens. Left a widow with a young daughter in her early twenties, she turned to nursing as a career, and studied under Florence Nightingale at St Thomas' Hospital in London. She was, in fact, the first nurse ever to take a patient's temperature, which she did with a thermometer two feet long! The mind boggles.

In 1873 Dr Robert Sinclair became Superintendent of Dundee Royal Infirmary (DRI), where he found a very unsatisfactory state of affairs with regard to nursing, especially among the night staff. He recommended the establishment of a training school for 'women of good character', and this was immediately approved by the directors. Rebecca Strong was appointed to carry out the plan. She came to Dundee as matron the following year and, with Dr Sinclair, set about providing the first nursing training in Scotland and transforming the service, setting standards for qualification world-wide.

At that time the average number of patients in DRI at any time was 100–130; in 1879 the total for the year was 1,735, of whom 78 were under 10 and only 104 over 60. She was in charge of 18 nurses (of whom 6 were probationers) and 19 servants, plus porters and firemen. In fact, the major part of her reforms seems to have been concerned with improving conditions. One of the first things she did was to put pictures on the walls of the wards. The directors provided help from a special fund to build new accommodation, pay was increased, working hours were reduced, and nurses were no longer required to do menial tasks. Probationers learned by being paired with qualified staff, and were given two hours' instruction a week from the Medical Superintendent. The effect of these improvements was stunning, and within four

years the nursing department was raised to an exceptionally high standard for its time. Nurses were remarked on for their "exceptional neatness", and the Directors noted: "...the combined gentleness and firmness... characteristic of the Matron, who treats the nurses and all the servants rather as sisters or daughters engaged with her in a benevolent work ... studying their welfare and appealing to that self-respect which establishes a high moral tone throughout the whole service" and creates "mutual good feeling and confidence, and a happy, cheerful spirit".

She moved on to Glasgow in 1879, but found little support for her ideas there until many years later. In 1907 she retired, but continued to devote herself whole-heartedly to the interests of nursing. She travelled the world broadcasting, and pursued her hobby of Alpine climbing. Only one return to Dundee is on record. She revisited DRI in 1929 to open a new Preliminary Training School for nurses. On her 96th birthday she was awarded the OBE; she lived on to just over 100.

Group of hospital staff outside DRI. Late 19th century.

Jean Thomson

1881 - 1940+

Jean Thomson has a good claim to be celebrated as Scotland's first policewoman. Some people wanted female police to protect women, and some wanted them to control women. Eventually the disruption of family life brought about by war in Europe triggered action and, in 1915, welfare-oriented Volunteer Women's Patrols were established in Dundee. Three years later the local branch of the National Union of Women Workers (who ran the Patrols) approached the Town Council's Police Committee to appoint Mrs Thomson as the first paid policewoman.

It seems the Chief Constable, John Carmichael, wasn't too keen on the idea, but he admitted that the Patrols "have been productive of good" and recommended Mrs Thomson's appointment as a 'police sister' for four hours a day. He pointed out, however, that until the Secretary for Scotland legalised the position of women police he would not be able to claim money for her, and he rather churlishly responded to the Patrols' request for uniform, hats and gloves by offering them hat badges. In 1922 he was to deny a policewoman had ever been on his strength.

Jean Forsyth Wright was born in 1881, the eldest child of the minister of Lochee Parish Church. At 21 she married a chemist, but he probably died while their three daughters were still young. She had been helping the police in a voluntary capacity for nine years before her appointment in 1918. Now she was given a half-allowance for her uniform and paid £60 a year to patrol the dance halls, cinemas and ice-cream parlours every evening. In fact she reported for duty every morning at nine and was on call all day, working with 'wayward girls and women' – interviewing, escorting, fetching home runaway girls, liaising with the RSSPCC and writing reports. She visited pubs too, but always with a male officer. She and her children lived with her widowed mother. She said she hardly ever saw them.

Mrs Thomson did not hold revolutionary views. All the same, when she gave evidence to the Baird Committee in 1920 about the role and status of women in policing, she was clear that a policewoman should be employed on the same footing as a man, paid on a par, and given power of arrest, in spite of all the arguments the Committee raised against this. "I would let her [a police woman] run the risk of getting hurt," she said. "It [the power of arrest] gives her a feeling of confidence; she knows that she is being backed".

Jean Thomson disappears from police statistics after December 1921, and possibly left Dundee altogether for a while. Later in life she lived in Albany Terrace and worked as a secretary for the Territorial Army. A woman colleague describes her as "tall, a wee bit daunting, just like you'd expect a policewomen to be - but good to work with". Jean Thomson, the second woman in Scotland to be employed in the police force, was the first whose duties really qualified her to be described as a policewoman. It was not until 1935 that the first official policewoman, Annie Ross, was appointed in Dundee.

MARY ALCOCK

1789 - 1869

Modern enterprise culture would be proud of the clever, successful, though rather eccentric Mary Ritchie. She was the daughter of a shoemaker and lived at 22 Barrack Street. When he died and left her property, she set up and ran a drapery business with Miss Jean Easson. Within twenty years she had made £10,000 - worth about £600,000 in 2008. So in 1827 she retired, saying that she had "made that muckle siller she was fear'd the Lord would turn against her". Aware that she was quite a catch in matrimonial terms, she had her lawyer prepare a marriage contract for her - with the name of the lucky man still a blank!

Then started the second half of her career, which she devoted, with great enjoyment, to litigation. She promptly embarked on a lawsuit against her former partner which went right up to the Court of Session. Although Miss Ritchie boasted that she never compromised, it is pleasant to record that Miss Easson was not bankrupted. Indeed she carried on the business at Barrack Street for at least another ten years. Around 1837 Miss Ritchie went down to Leamington to live, and there she met Mr R Alcock, a wood merchant. They married, but it was not a success. Within a few years she was back in Dundee, and taking him to court. She had "a keen nose for a lawyer", but if the lawyer wouldn't take up or continue a case she would promptly switch to another, and set him to suing his predecessor for her account.

In her lifetime she got through at least nine law firms. Although she was careful of the pennies and not easily imposed upon, she was also described as kind-hearted and charitable. In old age, she was a well-known figure round about the law courts, stooped and tottery and armed with her black bag and bundles of papers.

In later life, Mrs Alcock joined the Mormons. Although she kept saying she would make the pilgrimage to Utah, she never did and her bones lie not in the USA but in Dundee. It is not known who inherited the remainder of her considerable fortune.

Nineteenth century sketch of shops on Barrack Sreet.
Copyright © Dundee City Council, Local Studies Library, 2008

Victoria Drummond

1894 – 1978

Dundee Technical College (now the University of Abertay Dundee) helped many to qualify for practical careers. One of the most unusual was Victoria Alexandrina Drummond.

A god-daughter of Queen Victoria, she was born at Megginch Castle near Perth. Here she had a happy childhood, with trips to their London home and many family visits. She made butter and helped to tend animals and crops, but the farm machinery interested her most. Before she was twelve she was asking, "How can I learn to be an engineer and go to sea?" In 1916 Victoria became an apprentice in a Perth garage, studying for three evenings a week at the 'Tech'. In 1918 she moved to Lilybank Foundry, part of the Caledon Shipyard, then in 1922, fully qualified, she sailed for the first time on SS Anchises as 10th Engineer. She went to Australia four times on this coal-fired Blue Funnel liner cum cargo ship, then to Africa and India on the oil-fired TSS Mulbera.

Women were considered unlucky at sea, but influential contacts helped Victoria along. For example, on arrival in a foreign port she would crawl black and oily out of the engine room, and change into her cream satin dress to dine with local dignitaries. This tough, brave woman also loved shopping and embroidery and worried about her supply of henna shampoo. She spent the 1930s at home but in 1940 went to sea again, as 2nd Engineer on a Panamanian ship, SS Har Zion. The ship suffered a heavy air attack but Victoria shooed the crew out for their safety and single-handedly coaxed an extra three knots from the old engine, saving the ship. For this she was awarded an MBE and the Lloyds Medal for Bravery at Sea. In 1941 she saved another ship under attack. When all the engine crew scarpered in fear, Victoria chased them back to work.

She failed the British First Class Engineer's exam 41 times; the Board clearly did not want a female Chief. She trailed round shipping offices looking for a berth and when she got one she was paid less than the men. She did, however, gain a Panamanian Chief''s certificate and sailed on over 30 foreign ships, coping with small rust-buckets, many of them filthy, with bad food, drunken officers and criminal crews. She loved her job and kept a diary of her adventures. Victoria brought her last, dangerously leaky ship safely to harbour in 1962. She lived for some time with her sisters, and died in a nursing home after a long illness. There is a room named after her in the Institute of Marine Engineers, London.

SS Anchises, the first ship on which Victoria Drummond sailed.
Copyright © Scottish Maritime Museum, 2008. Licensor www.scran.ac.uk

KATHARINE READ

1723 – 1778

Y ou have probably heard of the eighteenth century painters Joshua Reynolds and Gainsborough. You are less likely to have heard of Katharine Read who, in her time, was just as well known and just as well paid.

Katharine Read was born in Logie into a comfortably-off family, the fifth child of Elizabeth Wedderburn and Alexander Read, a merchant. No one knows who taught her art, but certainly the family was friendly with Robert Strange the engraver, and by the time she was twenty two she had produced a very good painting of his relatives.

The family were also Jacobite sympathisers and in 1746 Katharine's uncle, John Wedderburn, was executed. A year earlier she had gone to France where she studied under pastellist, Marcel Quentin de la Tour. Later she studied in Italy for three years. Women in those days found art study difficult, for they were not allowed to attend public lectures or to draw from nature. Nonetheless, by this time Katharine was receiving pastel portrait commissions from both expatriates and Italians. People found her pictures soft, delicate, pleasing and good likenesses.

Back in London in 1754 Katharine set up her studio. She painted Queen Charlotte and her children, and was appointed 'Painter to the Queen'. Aristocrats and famous singers flocked to be painted by her, and she enjoyed considerable fame for the next twenty years, with her pictures often reproduced as engravings and mezzotints. In those days, visiting an artist's studio was a social occasion. The young writer Fanny Burney visited, and, while greatly admiring Katharine's work, had this to say: "Miss Read is shrewd and clever when she has any opportunity …but she is so very deaf. She is most exceedingly ugly, and of a very melancholic, or rather discontented humour...

... added to which she dresses in a style the most strange and queer that can be conceived".

Katharine, it appears, concentrated on her work and rather neglected her visitors and her appearance!

In 1777 she and her niece Helena sailed to India where she had a brother. Probably the first woman portraitist of nabobs, she had many commissions over the next three years. But Helena married and Katharine's health was fading. She set off for home, but died at sea. The fact that she painted mostly for private houses and seldom signed her work perhaps explains why this talented lady has been forgotten in Dundee.

Painting of society intellectual Elizabeth Carter, by Katharine Read. Commissioned by Elizabeth Montague (considered the leading literary hostess of her day). Reproduced by Courtesy of the Dr Johnson's House Trustees. Copyright © 2008

FLORENCE HORSBRUGH

1889 – 1969

The Unionist Party Headquarters once stood in Albert Square. Here was the work place of Florence Horsbrugh, the first and so far the only female Westminster MP for Dundee. She was also the first woman to move the address in reply to the King's Speech; first to be both a Privy Councillor and a Dame Grand Cross of the Order of the British Empire; first to be a Conservative cabinet minister; first to be a Fellow of the Royal College of Surgeons in Edinburgh. Yet Florence Horsbrugh came into politics almost by accident, when she stood in for an absent speaker at a meeting. Born into a middle-class Edinburgh family, she was 41 and already a MBE (for work in wartime canteens) when she was elected as a Unionist MP for Dundee, two years after all women over 21 got the vote. She said, if there were two MPs for Dundee, then it stood to reason that one should be a woman. She was to hold the seat continuously for fourteen years, until 1945.

She was a brilliant and attractive speaker, with a strong, deep voice, and was said to be one of the best-equipped party politicians of all the women in Parliament. Certainly she achieved a lot. In Dundee she set up trade agreements to help jute exports and successfully lobbied for the Caledon Shipyard to be put on the Admiralty List, thus much improving the employment situation. She successfully introduced two private member's bills, one curbing meths drinking in Scotland and the other regulating the adoption of children.

In 1939 she was appointed CBE and joined the Ministry of Health where, her interest in children continuing, she helped to organise evacuations from London. Towards the end of the war she did much preparatory work on the National Health scheme, which was later passed by the Labour Party. Defeated in Dundee in 1945, she returned to Parliament from a by-election in Moss Side, Manchester in 1950. The following year Winston Churchill made her Minister of

Education, a job which became a Cabinet post in 1953. She left the government the next year, but her public life continued, mostly on the international scene, where throughout her political career she led many a delegation to the League of Nations, the embryonic UN, UNESCO and the Council of Europe. Academic honours were heaped on her, and in 1959 she was created Baroness Horsbrugh.

Despite her rather severe appearance (she left off her glasses for the official photos) she was said to have been warm-hearted, interested in knitting patterns, humorous and a generous friend. "By her quiet example," the National Dictionary of Biography notes, "Florence Horsbrugh did much for the cause of women."

MARY LILY WALKER

1863 - 1913

I ncredible that hers is not a famous name! For Mary Lily Walker gathered an army of supporters about her, and transformed social conditions for poor families in Dundee. Her father, a Dundee solicitor, died when she was young and her mother was an invalid for whom she cared until her death in 1884. Nevertheless in 1883 Mary Lily Walker became one of University College's first woman entrants, where she studied Latin, Maths, Biology and Chemistry and was described as an excellent student.

A group of professors at the College, appalled by the social conditions of mill workers in the town, founded the Dundee Social Union (DSU), and Mary Lily Walker became one of its first and most enthusiastic members. "Leader" would perhaps be an appropriate word, except for the fact that, as one of her helpers explained: "It was only later that I realised that it was in her passion for clear and independent thinking that she would not use her influence directly, hoping for the emergence of initiative".

To learn more about how to do her job as Housing Superintendent for DSU she went to London, first to the Women's University Settlement, where she worked with Octavia Hill, and then to the Grey Ladies' Religious House. She wore a grey habit for the rest of her life. Returning to Dundee, she bought Walker House and founded Grey Lodge Settlement, the first settlement in Scotland and a 'centre for social work' from the day it began. One of her first jobs for DSU was to prepare, with Mona Wilson, detailed statistical reports on health and housing in Dundee, published in 1904. These revealed that 13-year-old elementary schoolgirls weighed nearly seven kilos less than their (average) English contemporaries, that 65% of houses fell below compulsory London standards, that 25% of houses had no toilets, at least not for women. Something had to be done. The dreadfully high infant mortality figures particularly concerned

her, so she opened restaurants for nursing mothers, helping them financially if they didn't return to work for three months (the fore-runner of maternity benefit?). Within five years infant mortality fell from 246 to 183 per 1,000. In the course of the next seven years, she also started baby clinics and home visiting of infants. Both functions were later taken on by the very enlightened Medical Officer of Health for Dundee, Dr Templeman. Dundee was the first city in Scotland to have a municipal infant health service.

Miss Walker helped open a hospital for women (later Elliot Road Hospital) in collaboration with Doctors Thomson and Moorhead (see plaque six). She started milk depots, school dinners and an after-school club. She opened a class for disabled children and raised funds for the bus to get them there. At Grey Lodge, girls' and boys' clubs flourished and the foundations for Dundee's nursery schools were laid. 1907 saw her Country Holiday and Recreation Committee gearing up to organise holidays for over 3,000 children. In her off-duty life, a friend said she was "able to put shop away with her Greyladies uniform", to entertain friends and pets in her cottage in Gauldry, Fife and go tramping in the Tyrol.

But there's more. Miss Walker did the preliminary work for the State Insurance Act, and was selected as a member of the Advisory Committee for Scotland. In 1913 she was commissioned to write another report for the government's Scottish Housing Committee. She was occupied with this, and with the opening of a first holiday camp in Elie, when she died. Right up until the end, she never lost her passionate concern for the poor or her capacity for innovation, and she never took 'no' for an answer.

Grey Lodge is in South George Street, and Walker House lies just behind it.

Left: Milne's Close, typical conditions in a Dundee tenement of the day
Copyright © Dundee City Council, Archives, 2008

MARY BROOKSBANK

1897 – 1978

"I have never had any personal ambitions. I have but one: to make my contribution to destroy the Capitalist system."

Born into an Aberdeen slum, the oldest of five children, Mary Soutar came to Dundee when she was eight or nine years old and started work in the mills at an illegal twelve. The foreman described her as "a richt wee smerter". Although she worked in various mills, she did not, in fact, work at Baxter's but she did write about it in the famous song.

Two years later, she had her first taste of what could be achieved by standing up to the bosses: the word went round the mills to follow "the lassie wi' the green felt hat", the mill girls marched, and they won a 15% rise. At twenty-one Mary rejected Roman Catholicism and shortly afterwards became an atheist and a member of the Communist Party, inspired by "Red" John McLean. She worked in various mills and various jobs, spent some time unemployed, and meanwhile went on demos, heckled, and was imprisoned several times for breach of the peace, for inciting riots or for "stating her beliefs in public". In the '30s, with thousands unemployed, demonstrations could draw crowds of 15,000, and Mary Brooksbank was right there in the middle. She joined a deputation of the National Unemployed Workers' Committee to talk with Churchill – a friendly enough meeting, if unproductive. She formed and led the Working Women's Guild and was also associated with the Railway Women's Guild. In 1933, she was expelled from the Communist Party for criticising Stalin – and also after an argument about whether the main body of the Party had taken the women's funds!

In the midst of this intensely political life, Mary remained part of a close-knit family, and her marriage to Ernest, a tailor, in 1924 simply added to the family circle. Family singsongs were a

A Dundee Lassie
(A Mill Song)

I'm a Dundee Lassie you can see
You'll aye find me cheerful
Nae maitter whar I be
Theres times I feel Doonhertec
Often Sad and Ill

    I'm a Spinner entae
     Baxters Mill

My Mither deed when I was young
My Father Fell in France
I'd a' liked tae been a Teacher
But I never got the chance
I'll soon be getting merriec
Tae a lad ca'd Tammy Hill

    He's an iler intae
     Halleys Mill

great entertainment, and Mary could both sing and play the violin. On one occasion, when there was no money left in the house, she took the ferry across to Tayport and sang in the streets. Her husband died in 1943, and she took in her parents and a nephew to live with her. Then, when she was about fifty, she finally gave up work to look after her sick mother and spent more time writing the poetry and songs that had always been part of her life. She did not entirely give up politics though, for she joined the Old Age Pensioners' Association, and became branch chairperson.

When the folk singer Ewan McColl commented on the shortage of songs about Dundee, Mary decided to disclose her poetry and writing. From then on her reputation grew. Her book of poems "Sidlaw Breezes", in Dundee's tradition of 19th century vernacular poetry, was published in 1966. She entertained in Old Folks' Clubs, sang at the Blairgowrie Music Festival and appeared on TV and radio. She also wrote her autobiography "No Sae Lang Syne" in which she set out her life-long manifesto for peace, equality and justice.

"When I was a young woman I was told I was a young woman in a hurry. Well, I'm an old woman now, and in a bigger hurry than ever!"

Brooksbank Centre in Mid Craigie is named in her honour. Baxter's Mill has been converted into housing at Weaver's Yard.

MARY SLESSOR

1848 – 1915

The tale of this mill-girl turned missionary has been told many times, but loses nothing in the telling. Stories abound of how this indomitable little woman set off into the jungles of Nigeria, often bare-foot and clad only in her petticoat, cropped red hair reflecting her fiery nature; how she said before she went: "I expect they will kill me," and was accustomed to part from the District Commissioner saying: "And see ye be a guid laddie!"

Mary was born in Aberdeen, one of seven children of a drunken father, but the family moved to Dundee for work when she was eleven, and she started part-time in Baxter's Mill, moving on to full-time flax weaving as soon as she was old enough.

Mother and children attended the Wishart Church and took a great interest in the activities of the United Presbyterian Mission in Calabar, Nigeria. Mary taught in Sunday School, and later in the Queen Street Mission, a tough area just round the corner, where she showed her own equal toughness. In 1875 she volunteered as a missionary, and set off the next year for Calabar, on a ship which carried, as she ruefully noted, "scores of casks [of rum] and just one missionary".

Calabar was then known as 'The White Man's Grave' because of its awful diseases and climate. Mary, in spite of coming from a sickly family and showing "a startling disregard for health or comfort" lived to be 67 - perhaps she simply hadn't time to die. From the comparative comforts of the principal town she moved further and further north-west, to places missionaries had never been before. In each place she established a base, then pressed on again, seeing herself as "the feet of God". Yet not all of her work, by any means, was missionary, and few Christians were baptised because of her.

Wherever she went Mary tended the sick, administered justice and fought against what she saw as the cruel customs of the tribes. For example, twins and their mothers were thrown into the jungle for the animals to eat; Mary saved them and took them into her own household. Many times she would save a victim (perhaps a woman due to be sacrificed at her husband's funeral) by sheer persistence: she simply sat beside the intended victim until everyone lost interest and went away.

She made friends with chieftains, notably King Edem and his widowed sister, Ma Eme. She worked with British administrators and was appointed a magistrate. She was "the uncrowned queen whose word was law". In between bouts of malaria, she cared for "her" children, cracked jokes, mended her mud house, tongue-lashed the unruly, set up schools and clinics and a settlement for women and girls and prayed to her friend God. In old age she was said to be thoroughly difficult, but she never lost a friend, and when she was buried in Duke Town her obituaries were so fulsome that one friend was moved to remark: "She was nae sae holy!"

By a strange turn of fate, Ma Eme's great-granddaughter is now married to a doctor from Dundee.

Mary Buick (or Buik)

1777 – 1854

Mary was born into a ropemaker's family, probably moderately well-off. When she was twenty she married a fisherman from Cellardyke, called Thomas Watson. He was a widower twelve years older than her; probably the man who, in January 1786, had told Kilrenny Kirk session that "maybe" he'd marry pregnant Margaret Thomson, did so, and fathered five children.

Shortly after marrying Mary, he was pressed into the navy and she contrived to be taken on as a nurse on board her husband's ship. Thomas did well and became a gunner and quartermaster. In April 1801 they were aboard the 64-gun ship HMS *Ardent* off Copenhagen, fighting what Vice-Admiral Nelson called 'the most terrific of all the 103 engagements he had been in', and the occasion when he put a telescope to his blind eye. In the midst of the battle Mary gave birth to her daughter Mary (sometimes called Margaret).

In 1803 Thomas was transferred to HMS *Victory* under the command of Nelson; Mary and little Mary went with him. Their ship was involved in many a fight; two years later came the battle of Trafalgar. Thomas was in charge of a gun crew and Mary tended the wounded while their daughter was kept out of harm's way below decks by another seaman from Cellardyke, Malcolm McRuvie. At the height of the battle, Nelson was killed. It was Mary, possibly with another woman called Mary Sperring, who later prepared his body for embalming. She would have undressed and washed him, cut off his hair, and then helped to lower him into a leaguer (a big cask) of brandy.

After the war Thomas got his discharge from the navy and used his prize money to open a pub in Cellardyke by the shore. Their house is now 7 Shore Street and, according to the occupiers in 2004, was built by the Watsons. Mary had several more children and outlived her husband by 23 years, living latterly with her grand-daughter. She was buried in Kilrennie churchyard in 1854. Her story has been handed down through the generations.

The Unicorn, upon which Mary's plaque can be found, was not built until shortly after Trafalgar but gives an idea of life on a fighting ship of the time.

HMS Victory leaving Portsmouth by Thomas Elliot
Copyright © National Trust for Scotland, 2008. Licensor www.scran.ac.uk

BELLA KEYZER

1922 – 1992

"I 'll be as tough as the bloody rest of them!" said big Bella Keyzer. She was a woman in a man's world – a shipyard welder – and she worked among towering cranes. Born Bella Mitchell, she was the youngest of five children. The family lived in Charles Street. Her father, a baker, was a committed trade unionist . He was imprisoned during the General Strike and politics was part of the family's daily bread. Her mother, though she seldom went out to work, was kept busy at home, especially when two refugee girls from the Spanish Civil War joined the household. Bella described herself as a child as 'a harum-scarum bitch'; she once took a swipe at a teacher who (she thought) had called her mother lazy.

By the time she was 15 she was working – in a cafe, in a nursing home, folding bags, weaving canvas, never long in one place. Then in 1941, at the Empress Ballroom, she met her future husband Dirk, a seaman in the Dutch Navy. She became pregnant, but because he was frequently posted elsewhere it was 1949 before they actually married.

Meanwhile, Granny minded the little boy while Bella worked, first in a munitions factory and then as a welder at Bonar Long, and later in Caledon Shipyard (where the pay was 2/6d more), along with perhaps 20 other women 'drafted in' for the war. She was a big, strong woman though, she said, 'every inch feminine', and she had found the job she loved. The men accepted the women workers because they knew they would be gone after the war. Although women had only temporary union cards and were not allowed to attend meetings, the boilermakers' union backed Bella and her co-worker Jessie when they asked for a rise to come nearer the men's pay, and they won £1 per week. After the war, the women were paid off without notice and Bella went on the trams, but she longed to go back to the yards. She applied for various jobs, signing herself only "I" instead of "Isabel" – but she never got past the interview! "I'm afraid, my dear,

~ 54 ~

you're a woman," was the typical response. She spent a few years in Holland, where she found the women very subservient. "When you spoke to the women it was 'Meh man said this and meh man said that'. I said 'Never mind what yer bloody man said, what the hell do you say?'"

Back in Dundee, she did 'women's work', finding a quite different atmosphere in a pally women's factory but also becoming aware of the problems women workers faced – "It got right up my nose."

Finally, when the Equal Opportunities Act was passed in 1975, Bella returned to the shipyards, the only female employee. She got a warm (though surprised) welcome, her own toilet and permission to leave four minutes early in order not to be caught in the rush. Her male-type life left her something of a misfit with 'womanly' women, but her cheery nature and native shrewdness stood her in good stead, and her work gave her a sense of identity and pride. She would have loved to launch a ship: "That's my work. If they were going to ask a woman they should have asked me ... The ships are beautiful and I'm as beautiful as the queen, because I made something".

Bella appeared in a number of TV programmes in the 1980s, and in 1992 Dundee District Council gave her a special award for her work to promote women's equality. She was a faithful member of the Labour Party; even in her last illness she insisted on being fetched from hospital and driven to the polling booth. She said of her life: "I think for women's equality I threw a small pebble in the water. It was a very, very small wave, but it was my wave, and I feel I achieved something".

Although the shipyards have long gone, her plaque overlooks the river where the Caledon ships were launched.

Women working on ship propellor c.1940.
Reproduced with kind permission from Zoo Design

Ethel Moorhead

1869 - 1955

Ethel Moorhead has a double claim to fame - as the finest Dundee woman artist of her time and as, if not the leader, then certainly the "most turbulent" of Dundee's suffragettes. Her studio was in the King Street Arcade, which ran from King Street up to Victoria Road but has now vanished under the ring road.

Ethel was Alice's (See plaque six) younger sister, the daughter of an army surgeon, brought up in India and other parts of the Empire. In contrast to her pretty sister she was described as "handsome" though not robust. She studied art in Paris under Mucha and at Whistler's studio, coming occasionally to Dundee, where she shared the studio with a Miss Oliphant. The first paintings she exhibited at Dundee Graphic Arts Society (in 1901) were said to be "the gems of the collection", "notable for their dark tones and strength of colour".

A couple of years later her parents and younger brother arrived in Dundee, and Ethel went home to act as housekeeper, but she kept her portrait painting business in the Arcade. She exhibited widely, with (amongst other shows) eight pictures at the Royal Scottish Academy and four at the Glasgow Institute.

In 1910 her sister Alice died and her father died the following year. By this time Ethel had become a member of the Dundee branch of the Women's Social & Political Union. Proclaiming "No vote, no tax!" she allowed a candelabra to be poinded from the family home in lieu of payment, then off she went to the auction in the Greenmarket and bought it back, teasing the auctioneer unmercifully with ridiculous bids and raising cheers from the sympathetic crowd. She moved to Edinburgh to continue painting, but this didn't stop her campaigning for votes. She was to be found, under various aliases, smashing glass in Stirling, attacking an opponent

with a dog whip in Edinburgh, causing a disturbance in Aberdeen, throwing pepper and water over policemen in Fife and then showing her contempt for the court proceedings by refusing to stand or to remove her veil for identification. This last offence brought her her heaviest sentence so far - thirty days' imprisonment. By the time she reached Perth Prison she had already been fasting for four days and because the doctor was reluctant to force-feed her, she was released after two days.

Undaunted, she had a go at arson in Glasgow. (Farington Hall in Dundee, which was burnt down by an unknown arsonist, was also suspiciously close to the Moorheads' house!) Sentenced to eight months, she was released under the Cat & Mouse Act, and escaped recapture for four months.

This time she really was force-fed, the first woman in Scotland to undergo such treatment. There were demos and deputations on her behalf by the suffragettes, but the prison doctor remarked, "...I have been far too frequently threatened by lunatics in and out of prison to worry about this lot". She was released on licence, suffering from pneumonia, and it was about this time that she left Dundee for good, selling her house to another artist.

During World War One she kept on painting, exhibiting in Dublin and London as well as in Scotland. By the mid-1920s she had settled in Paris, where, wearing a plaid suit and pince nez, she wrote, drew and co-edited a well-regarded arts magazine, "This Quarter". Nothing is known of her latter years, but she certainly returned to Ireland, where she is buried in an unmarked grave. A sad end for such a talented, intelligent, spirited and courageous woman.

Left: Sketch of Ethel Moorhead with her dog, Pine Tree.

GRISSELL JAFFRAY

? – 1669

Forget the idea of a wild-haired hag from 'Macbeth'. Grissell Jaffray was the wife of a respectable burgess of the city of Dundee who had the misfortune to live at a time when fear of witches was at its height. Witches had been burned in Dundee a hundred years before, for the edification of Regent Moray when he visited, but the persecution increased under the reign of Charles II.

We don't know when Grissell Jaffray was born, but her husband James Butchart (women in those days usually kept their own surnames) was born in 1594, so she must have been in her 60s or 70s at the time of her death. According to tradition she was a simple countrywoman from Aberdeenshire, but more recent research has revealed that she and her husband were rich enough to make loans of over £3,000. It is possible, too, that she was a relation of Provost Jaffray of Aberdeen, a notable Quaker.

The couple lived in Calendar Close, off Long Wynd. They had one child and James plied a successful trade as a brewer. Then disaster struck. She was arrested and imprisoned in the Tolbooth in November 1669, charged with "the horrid crime of witchcraft", which may have amounted to no more than telling fortunes or predicting the weather – perhaps the country lore she learned in childhood was regarded as witchcraft by town-dwellers. Or did religious differences come into it?

Under torture she confessed (wouldn't you?) and was sentenced and burned at the stake some time before the 23rd of the month. The relevant court records were destroyed. It has been suggested there was a cover-up, given that witches were supposed to be banished, not burned, but the names of the three ministers responsible are on record. They were all leading ministers in the Dundee Presbytery at the time: Harry Scrymsour of St Mary's, John Guthrie of South Church and William Rait of Third Charge, now St Paul's.

The story goes that she was burned in the Seagate but it is likely that the execution actually took place in one of the long fields leading down towards the river from the Seagate, away from the town centre, lest the wooden houses go up in flames as well as the victim. At this point folklore really takes over. It is said that Grissell's son, James the younger, returning from a sea voyage, saw the smoke rising above the town and asked what caused it. When he was told, he turned his ship and left Dundee for ever. Fate was not kind to the elder James Butchart either, only ten days after his wife was burnt he applied, destitute, for admittance to the Poor House. Did the couple have some spiteful enemy? Or had he spent all his money in fruitless legal fees?

Grissell Jaffray was the last witch to be burned in Dundee, but not the last to be accused, for two were thrown out of the town the following spring. The last execution of a British witch was at Dornoch in 1722.

We should not delude ourselves that fear of witchcraft is all in the past. Former Dundee jute mill worker Helen Duncan was tried under the Witchcraft Act for "pretending to be a medium" as recently as 1944. She was jailed for nine months. A spiritualist, Helen somehow revealed the deaths of servicemen before these had been officially reported - unnerving in a time of strict censorship.

Mosaic in Peter Street symbolising the flames
Copyright © GSR Photographic, 2008

JANET KEILLER

1737 - 1813

Dundee is renowned for 'jam, jute and journalism'; Mrs Keiller provided the jam. Once upon a time, there was a Dundee grocer/confectioner called John who, one day when he was old enough to know better, was conned by a Spanish shipmaster into buying a consignment of Seville oranges. Nobody wanted them. It looked as if they would be left to rot until, it is said, Mrs Keiller set to in her kitchen and boiled them up to make marmalade. Jams had previously been made by pulping the fruit, but she cut it up, thus producing the first 'chip' marmalade.

The new product was a great success and took its place beside the cakes and sweeties. In 1797, when she and John were sixty, Janet set up in business with her son James, trading initially as 'James Keiller' and changing to 'James Keiller & Son' in 1804. The '& Son' was certainly appropriate, for James had at least eight sons (and eight daughters), though it seems most of them died young. Three of his sons by his second wife, Margaret Spence, were to carry on the family tradition. However, James died when the boys were still young, and it was left to his widow Margaret to carry on the business. Thus she became the second Keiller woman to make a significant contribution to the family fortunes. The business began at the top of the Seagate, which in those days (before more land was reclaimed) was near to the port and to a sugar refinery. In 1850 Margaret organised a move to a shop in Castle Street with a factory nearby, and business boomed. Two of the sons, now grown up, opened works in the tax haven of Guernsey. A big Keiller factory which opened about 1870 remained in Albert Square until 1972. Keiller is a name world-wide - but would the men have managed it on their own?

Right: Jam-making pans in Keiller's factory.
Copyright © Dundee City Council, Local Studies Library, 2008

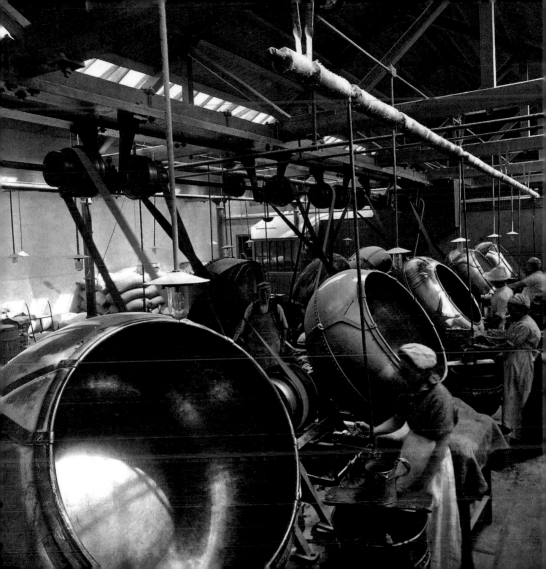

Emma Caird (or Marryat)

1849 - 1927

It's not only architects and builders who shape the face of a city: someone has to put up the money. One of those who did so was Mrs Marryat, who was described as "the greatest benefactress Dundee has ever seen". Born Emma Caird, she was the youngest daughter of Edward Caird of Loch Long, Dumbartonshire, and half-sister of Sir James Caird, owner of one of Dundee's most prosperous jute mills. She and James were, it seems, very close, and they travelled the world together - to Berlin for the Kaiser's wedding, then on to St Petersburg (at which time Czar Alexander II was assassinated), Moscow, Odessa and Vienna. On another occasion, they visited the USA, crossing the Rockies by stagecoach and going on to Japan. Emma made friends with Robert E. Lee, and with Whistler's mother. She was a fearless horsewoman - though less successful on a bicycle!

In 1892, at the age of 43, she married Lt Col Herbert Marryat (retd) of the Manchester Regiment. This big game hunter of Kashmir now settled down, and the couple lived between Ireland and a Scottish property given to Emma by her brother. Her only daughter died as an infant. Then, in 1916/17, her half-brother and her husband died within eighteen months of each other. James had long before willed all his lands and investments to his sister, and now she moved into his house in Roseangle and spent the last ten years of her life giving away a fortune.

She gave to Dundee Royal Infirmary, donated Belmont Estate as (initially) a rest home for disabled soldiers and gave money to complete the building of the Caird Hall, where the smaller hall is named after her. Altogether she and her brother gave £400,000 to Dundee, nearly half of it in that last decade. In 1918 she was made a burgess of this city, the fourth woman to be so honoured. She died at the age of 78, and her portrait hangs in the Caird Hall foyer. However it is a measure of how unimportant women were still considered to be that her obituary gives a list, not of her donations but of those of her brother, the long-deceased Sir James.

Painting of Emma Caird by David Foggie.
Copyright © Dundee City Council, 2008

More

to see and read ...

Verdant Works is a jute mill museum in West Henderson's Wynd, Dundee; you can see and hear working machinery, listen to recordings of former jute mill workers and see where the children of the weavers and spinners lived and went to school. (www.rrsdiscovery.com)

Frigate Unicorn is on the Women's Trail at City Quay; go below decks on this authentic sailing ship and imagine Mary Buick dressing wounds in the frantic chaos of a battle at sea. (www.frigateunicorn.org)

Dundee Central Library's Local History section has a wealth of material about the city and its people. The Library is in the Wellgate Centre just off Victoria Road. (www.dundeecity.gov.uk)

Find out more at **www.dundeewomenstrail.org.uk**

Dundee Women's Trail is co-ordinated by Jean Annand, Kate Armstrong, Moira Foster, Mary Henderson and Edith Hamilton.

ACKNOWLEDGEMENTS

The idea for this book and companion trail came from members of Engender (www.engender.org.uk) a national organisation for women in Scotland. Mary Henderson and Olive Smiles began to work on it in 1997, but although heritage groups and Dundee City Council were enthusiastic no-one was able to commit the necessary funds to establish the trail as a permanent fixture and publish the book. A modest photocopied booklet sold well and talks were given to women's groups all over Tayside, and in 2003 Dundee Rep staged a dramatised version, but funding remained elusive. Then, in November of that year, Dundee Women's Trail established a Committee and became a registered charity. Over the next two years Committee members Jean Annand (Chair), Mary Henderson (Secretary), Kate Armstrong (Treasurer), Edith Hamilton and Moira Foster took on the responsibility of preparing a Heritage Lottery Fund application and subsequently managed the project when a generous grant was awarded by HLF to enable the casting of the plaques, printing of the book and construction of the website. This Project Management Team secured further funding from the City of Discovery Campaign and a commitment from Dundee City Council that they would take over responsibility for the maintenance of the Trail in due course. So ten years on, here we are!

Each woman in this book has her own numbered plaque. Guided walks happen from time to time as part of International Women's Week or the Urban Walking Festival but it's easy to Do-It-Yourself; a pleasant walk on a fine day. When it rains, just curl up and read this book indoors.

Thanks are due to the most helpful staff at the Local History Department of the Central Library including David Kett and Eileen Moran. Thanks must also go to: Stewart Murdoch and Moira Methven, Leisure and Communities; Iain Flett and Richard Cullen, City Archives; Clara Young and Eileen Murison, McManus Galleries; Gill Poulter, Dundee Heritage Trust; Lesley Lindsay, University of Dundee; Stuart Syme, School Library Service; Economic Development Department, especially Michael McLaughlin; Tayside Police Archives; University of Dundee Archives; DC Thomson & Co Ltd.; Ron Grosset of Geddes and Grosset; Liz Small, Publishing Scotland; Louise Wilson, Booksource.

Over the years support has come notably from Christine Lowden (DVA), Merv Rolfe, Jill Shimi and many other officials. We are grateful to all the proprietors who agreed to have plaques on their walls, many of whom also supported our Lottery application, and to a hundred friends who contributed useful information and encouragement.

Thanks also to Jimmy Black and Julie Bell who helped to co-ordinate the project at different stages. We have been very fortunate to work with Su Nicoll @ Zoo Design and Colin Keillor of Keillor Graphics..

Thank you, one and all!
Dundee Women's Trail Committee, 2008

Short Bibliography

Contemporary quotes are taken from the newspapers of the day and are also drawn from the following sources:

Biographical Dictionary of Scottish Women   ed. Ewan, Innes et al (2006) Edinburgh University Press
Dictionary of National Biography   (2004), Oxford University Press
Bonnie Fechters: Women in Scotland 1900-50   Sheila Livingstone (1994), Scottish Library Association
Dundee at Work   J. Murray (1995), Alan Sutton Publishing Ltd
Dundee, its Life & Times   Whatley, Swinfen & Smith (1993), John Donald Publishers Ltd
Dundee Worthies   Comp. George Martin (1934), David Winter & Sons
Juteopolis: Dundee & its Textile Workers 1885-1923   William M. Walker (1979), Scottish Academic Press
Miles tae Dundee   Janice Murray & D. Stockdale (1990), Dundee Art Galleries and Museums
The Re-making of Juteopolis   ed. Christopher A Whately (1992), Abertay Historical Society
The Scotswoman at Home and Abroad   ed. Dorothy McMillan (1999), ASLS
The Scottish Suffragettes   Leah Leneman (2000), NMS Publishing
Victorian Dundee – Image & Realities   Miskell, Whately & Harris (2000), Tuckwell Press
Daughters of Dundee   Norman Watson (1997), Linda McGill

EASY READING

The Expendable Mary Slessor   James Buchan (1980), St Andrews Press
The Book of Marmalade   Anne Wilson (1985), Constable
Female Tars   Suzanne Stark (1998), Pimlico

These books are available at the Local History Library, Wellgate Library, Dundee. A fuller bibliography is available on the website at www.dundeewomenstrail.org.uk